inspiration
for a
lifetime

inspiration *for a* lifetime

Words of Wisdom, Delight and Possibility

COMPILED BY ALLEN KLEIN
FOREWORD BY BJ GALLAGHER

EDITIONS

Published in the United States by Viva Editions, an imprint of Cleis Press Inc., 2246 Sixth Street, Berkeley CA 94710.

Printed in the United States.
Cover design: Scott Idleman
Cover photograph: Image Source
Text design: Frank Wiedemann
First Edition.
10 9 8 7 6 5 4 3 2 1

Library of Congress Cataloging-in-Publication Data

Inspiration for a lifetime : words of wisdom, delight and possibility / Compiled by Allen Klein ; foreword by B.J. Gallagher.
    p. cm.
 Includes index.
 ISBN 978-1-57344-429-3 (alk. paper)
1. Conduct of life--Quotations, maxims, etc. I. Klein, Allen.
BJ1581.2.I54 2010
081--dc22
                                    2010038192

For all the great teachers in my life,
who inspired me and enriched my life.

CONTENTS

I've always loved inspiring quotes—they provide timeless wisdom, previous pearls of encouragement, and hope. The right quote at the right time can make the difference between a day of despair and a day of delight. It's funny how just a few words—uttered or written by someone you've never met—can have such a big impact.

Words are powerful; words create worlds; words provide nourishment for the psyche and sustenance for the soul. Words can warm our hearts. . .or move us to tears. Words can fire us up to take on the world. . .or calm us down when we're stressed or distressed.

In this book, *Inspiration for a Lifetime*, Allen Klein has gathered a marvelous collection of words to live by, words to love by, words to laugh by. I'm delighted that some of my favorites are included—and happy to discover some new quotes I'd never seen before. This book is a veritable *feast* of fine inspiration. Dig in!

BJ Gallagher
Author of *It's Never Too Late to Be What You Might Have Been*

INTRODUCTION

The quotations in this book are sometimes wise, sometimes witty, but they are always inspirational.

When they are wise, they can lend a hand in helping you overcome your tough times. And when they are witty, they will give you a different view of your solemn situation—and nothing, perhaps, gives a better perspective than a good laugh.

In either case, pick this book up when you or someone you know needs some uplifting encouragement. One reader, for example, told me that each day she emailed a quote from the book to her ailing mother. She said it not only cheered her mother up but selecting them helped her too.

The quotations in this book focus on trying times, such

as "aging," "diet and exercise," "raising kids," etc. They were designed to be used in a variety of ways:

- ⚙ Pick up the book, randomly open to a quote, and let those words be your guiding thought for the day or the week.
- ⚙ Use these quotes as you would any reference book—in speeches, on bulletin boards, in newsletters, in your emails, etc.
- ⚙ Read a section at a time and savor its wit and wisdom.

However you use these wonderful words, my hope is that the inspiring quotations in this book will provide you with a lesson or a laugh for not only the moment, but for a lifetime.

Allen Klein, San Francisco
www.allenklein.com

A quotation at the right
moment is like bread
in a famine.

THE TALMUD

A

AGE & AGING

age *v* the length of time that one has existed
ag•ing *n* the process of growing old or maturing

Age is a question of mind over matter.
If you don't mind, it doesn't matter.

SATCHEL PAIGE

I was born in 1962. True.
And the room next to me was 1963.

JOAN RIVERS

I'm not interested in age.
People who tell their age are silly.
You're as old as you feel.

ELIZABETH ARDEN

Age is not important unless you're a cheese.

HELEN HAYES

The prime of life is that fleeting time
between green and over-ripe.

CULLEN HIGHTOWER

My mother always used to say:
"The older you get, the better you get,
unless you're a banana."
ROSE NYLUND IN "THE GOLDEN GIRLS"

Wisdom doesn't automatically come with old age.
Nothing does—except wrinkles.
It's true, some wines improve with age,
but only if the grapes were good in the first place.
ABIGAIL VAN BUREN

Old age isn't so bad when you consider the alternative.
MAURICE CHEVALIER

The secret of staying young is to live honestly,
eat slowly, and lie about your age.
LUCILLE BALL

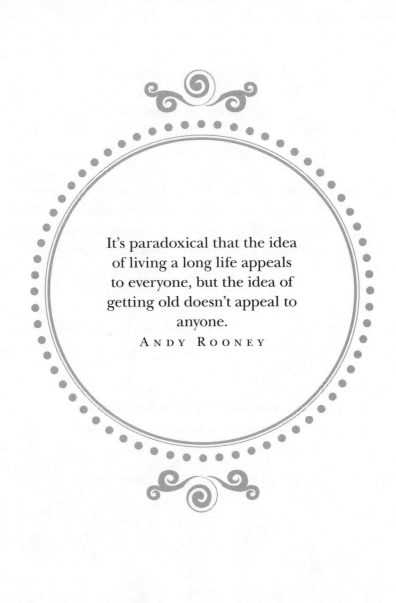

It's paradoxical that the idea
of living a long life appeals
to everyone, but the idea of
getting old doesn't appeal to
anyone.

ANDY ROONEY

Thirty-five is a very attractive age.
London society is full of women
of the highest birth who have, of their own free choice,
remained thirty-five for years.

OSCAR WILDE

Life begins at forty.

WALTER B. PITKIN

To be seventy years young is sometimes
far more cheerful
and hopeful than to be forty years old.

OLIVER WENDELL HOLMES

I've always roared with laughter when they say life begins
at forty. That's the funniest remark ever.
The day I was born was when life began for me.

BETTE DAVIS

A woman past forty
should make up her mind to be young—not her face.

B I L L I E   B U R K E

Now that I'm over sixty
I'm veering toward respectability.

S H E L L E Y   W I N T E R S

I'm over the hill, but the climb was terrific!

G R A F F I T I

Just remember, once you're over the hill,
you begin to pick up speed.

C H A R L E S   S C H U L Z

Old age is like a plane flying through a storm.
Once you're aboard, there's nothing you can do.

G O L D A   M E I R

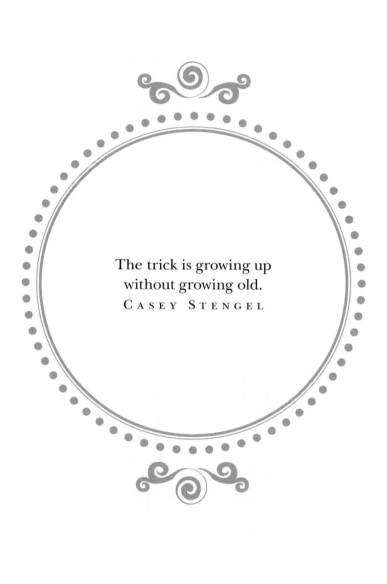

The trick is growing up
without growing old.

CASEY STENGEL

You can't help getting older,
but you don't have to get old.

GEORGE BURNS

If you carry your childhood with you,
you never become older.

ABRAHAM SUTZKEVER

Whatever a man's age may be,
he can reduce it several years
by putting a bright-colored flower in his buttonhole.

MARK TWAIN

When it comes to staying young,
a mind-lift beats a face-lift any day.

MARTY BUCELLA

Everyone is the age of their heart.

GUATEMALAN SAYING

We are always the same age inside.
GERTRUDE STEIN

I'll tell ya how to stay young:
Hang around with older people.
BOB HOPE

Being middle-aged is a nice change
from being young.
DOROTHY CANFIELD FISHER

Middle age is when you've met so many people
that every new person you meet
reminds you of someone else.
OGDEN NASH

Middle age is when your age starts
to show around your middle.
BOB HOPE

Don't worry about middle age: you'll outgrow it.
LAURENCE J. PETER

You know you are getting old when people tell you
how good you look.
ALAN KING

You know you are getting old when the candles
cost more than the cake.
BOB HOPE

I smoke cigars because at my age
if I don't have something to hang onto
I might fall down.
GEORGE BURNS

I have everything now that I had twenty years ago—
except now it's all lower.
GYPSY ROSE LEE

They tell you that you'll lose your mind
when you grow older. What they don't tell you
is that you won't miss it very much.

MALCOLM COWLEY

There are three signs of old age. Loss of memory. . .
I forget the other two.

RED SKELTON

My grandfather's a little forgetful,
but he likes to give me advice.
One day, he took me aside and left me there.

RON RICHARDS

First you forget names,
then you forget faces,
then you forget to pull your zipper up,
then you forget to pull your zipper down.

LEO ROSENBERG

My dad's pants kept creeping up on him.
By sixty-five he was just a pair of pants and a head.
JEFF ALTMAN

One of the many pleasures of old age is giving things up.
MALCOLM MUGGERIDGE

I look forward to being older,
when what you look like becomes less and less an issue
and what you are is the point.
SUSAN SARANDON

There is many a good tune played on an old fiddle.
OLD SAYING

There is a fountain of youth;
it is your mind, your talents, the creativity you bring to
your life and the lives of the people you love. When you
learn to tap this source, you will have truly defeated age.
SOPHIA LOREN

I never feel age. . . .
If you have creative work, you
don't have age or time.
Louise Nevelson

I want to tell people approaching and
perhaps fearing age that it is a time of discovery.
If they say, "Of what?" I can only answer
"We must find out for ourselves,
otherwise it won't be discovery."
F L O R I D A   S C O T T - M A X W E L L

Anyone can get old.
All you have to do is live long enough.
G R O U C H O   M A R X

How old would you be if you didn't
know how old you were?
S A T C H E L L   P A I G E

Don't complain about growing old—
many people don't have that privilege.
E A R L   W A R R E N

A

ANGER & ADVERSITY

an•ger *n* a strong feeling of hostility or displeasure
ad•ver•si•ty *n* a state of hardship or distress

This makes me so sore it gets my dandruff up.
S A M U E L   G O L D W Y N

The best remedy for a short temper is a long walk.
J A C Q U E L I N E   S C H I F F

Anyone can become angry. That is easy. But to be angry
with the right person, to the right degree, at the right
time, for the right purpose, and in the right way—that is
not easy.
A R I S T O T L E

As a girl my temper often got out of bounds.
But one day when I became angry at a friend over some
trivial matter, my mother said to me,
"Elizabeth, anyone who angers you conquers you."
S I S T E R   E L I Z A B E T H   K E N N Y

The greatest remedy for anger is delay.
S E N E C A

Grow angry slowly—there's plenty of time.
RALPH WALDO EMERSON

Speak when you are angry
and you will make the best speech you will ever regret.
AMBROSE BIERCE

Getting angry can sometimes be like leaping into a
wonderfully responsive sports car, gunning the motor,
taking off at high speed,
and then discovering the brakes are out of order.
MAGGIE SCARF

To rule one's anger is well; to prevent it is still better.
TRYON EDWARDS

If you are patient in one moment of anger,
you will escape a hundred days of sorrow.
CHINESE SAYING

It is impossible for you to be
angry and laugh at the same
time. Anger and laughter are
mutually exclusive,
and you have the power to
choose either.

WAYNE DYER

There are two ways of meeting difficulties:
you alter the difficulties,
or you alter yourself to meet them.
PHYLLIS BOTTOME

We win half the battle when we make up our minds
to take the world as we find it, including the thorns.
ORISON S. MARDEN

Drag your thoughts away from your troubles—
by the ears, by the heels, or any other way you can
manage it. It's the healthiest thing a body can do.
MARK TWAIN

When the first Superman movie came out I was
frequently asked, "What is a hero?" My answer was that
a hero is someone who commits a courageous action
without considering the consequences. . . . Now my
definition is completely different. I think a hero is an
ordinary individual who finds strength to persevere and
endure in spite of overwhelming obstacles.

CHRISTOPHER REEVE

The happy and efficient people in this world are those
who accept trouble as a normal detail of human life
and resolve to capitalize it when it comes along.

H. BERTRAM LEWIS

Problems are only opportunities in work clothes.

HENRY J. KAISER

You seek problems because you need their gifts.

RICHARD BACH

Everything that irritates us about others can lead us to an
understanding of ourselves.

CARL JUNG

Heartbreak is life educating us.

GEORGE BERNARD SHAW

I learned long ago never to wrestle with a pig.
You get dirty, and besides, the pig likes it.

CYRUS CHING

When things are bad, we take comfort in the thought
that they could always be worse. And when they are, we
find hope in the thought that things are so bad they have
to get better.

MALCOLM FORBES

When I hear somebody sigh, "Life is hard,"
I am always tempted to ask, "Compared to what?"

SYDNEY J. HARRIS

When life's problems seem overwhelming,
look around and see what other people are coping with.
You may consider yourself fortunate.

ANN LANDERS

When you dig another out of their troubles,
you find a place to bury your own.

ANONYMOUS

The human capacity to fight back will always astonish
doctors and philosophers. It seems, indeed, that there
are no circumstances so bad and no obstacles so big that
man cannot conquer them.

JEAN TETREAU

The bitterest misfortune can be covered up with a smile.

YIDDISH SAYING

He knows not his own strength
that hath not met adversity.

BEN JONSON

Without adversity, without change, life is boring.
The paradox of comfort is that we stop trying.
JOHN AMATT

Take chances, make mistakes. That's how you grow.
Pain nourishes your courage.
You have to fail in order to practice being brave.
MARY TYLER MOORE

Although the world is full of suffering,
it also full of the overcoming of it.
HELEN KELLER

You don't have to suffer.
JUDY TATELBAUM

One of the secrets of life
is to make stepping stones out of stumbling blocks.
JACK PENN

The worst thing in your life
may contain seeds of the best.
When you can see crisis as an opportunity,
your life becomes not easier, but more satisfying.

JOE KOGEL

What is to give light must endure burning.

VIKTOR FRANKL

If we had no winter, the spring would not be so pleasant.
If we did not sometimes taste of adversity,
prosperity would not be so welcome.

ANNE BRADSTREET

He who can't endure the bad will not live to see the good.

YIDDISH SAYING

The way I see it, if you want the rainbow,
you gotta put up with the rain.
DOLLY PARTON

If we fight against the waves that pass over us in life,
we are overpowered. If we move with the waves in life
as they roll over us, the wave passes on.

PESIKTA ZURTARTI

Expect trouble as an inevitable part of life
and repeat to yourself the most comforting words of all:
This, too, shall pass.

ANN LANDERS

C

CHANGE & CHALLENGE

change *v* to cause to be different
chal•lenge *n* a test of one's abilities
in a demanding undertaking

It's always something.
GILDA RADNER

There is nothing permanent except change.
HERACLITUS

Everything is changing.
People are taking their comedians seriously
and the politicians as a joke.
WILL ROGERS

The more things change,
the more they remain the same.
ALPHONSE KARR

Even if you're on the right track,
you'll get run over if you just sit there.
WILL ROGERS

It seems necessary to completely shed the old skin
before the new, brighter, stronger,
more beautiful one can emerge…
I never thought I'd be getting a life lesson from a snake.

JULIE RIDGE

Should you shield the canyons from the windstorms,
you would never see the beauty of their carvings.

ELISABETH KÜBLER-ROSS

To keep our faces toward change and behave like free
spirits in the presence of fate is strength undefeatable.

HELEN KELLER

Happy is he who learns to bear what he cannot change.

J. C. F. VON SCHILLER

If matters go badly now, they will not always do so.

HORACE

Perhaps one day this too will be pleasant to remember.
V I R G I L

In spite of illness, in spite even of the
archenemy sorrow, one can remain alive
long past the usual date of disintegration if one is
unafraid of change, insatiable in intellectual curiosity,
interested in big things, and happy in small ways.
E D I T H   W H A R T O N

Changes are not only possible and predictable,
but to deny them is to be an accomplice to one's
own unnecessary vegetation.
G A I L   S H E E H Y

We cannot change anything unless we accept it.
C A R L   J U N G

If you can't change your fate, change your attitude.
A M Y   T A N

A positive attitude may not
solve all your problems,
but it will annoy enough
people to make it worth the
effort.

HERM ALBRIGHT

Life is change. Growth is optional. Choose wisely.
KAREN KAISER CLARK

When you're through changing, you're through.
BRUCE BARTON

If you realize that all things change,
there is nothing you will try to hold onto.
TAO TE CHING

A permanent state of transition is man's most noble
condition.
JUAN RAMON JIMENEZ

Consistency is contrary to nature, contrary to life.
The only completely consistent people are the dead.
ALDOUS HUXLEY

If you fear change, leave it here.
SIGN ON A RESTAURANT TIP JAR

You learn more from ten days of agony
than from ten years of content.
SALLY JESSY RAPHAEL

So often we try to alter circumstances to suit ourselves,
instead of letting them alter us,
which is what they are meant to do.
MOTHER MARIBEL

I have always grown from my problems and challenges,
from things that don't work out;
that's when I've really learned.
CAROL BURNETT

The hardships of life are sent not by an
unkind destiny to crush, but to challenge.
SAM E. ROBERTS

The ultimate measure of a man is not where he stands
in moments of comfort and convenience, but where he
stands at times of challenge and controversy.
MARTIN LUTHER KING, JR.

Sometimes things which at the moment may be perceived
as obstacles—and actually be obstacles, difficulties, or
drawbacks—can in the long run result in some good end
which would not have occurred if it
had not been for the obstacle.
STEVE ALLEN

God gave burdens, also shoulders.
YIDDISH SAYING

That which does not kill me
makes me stronger.

FRIEDRICH NIETZSCHE

We all have to go through the tumbler a few times
before we can emerge as a crystal.

ELISABETH KÜBLER-ROSS

The gem cannot be polished without friction,
nor man perfected without trials.

CHINESE SAYING

Everyone gets their rough day. No one gets a free ride.
Today so far, I had a good day. I got a dial tone.

RODNEY DANGERFIELD

I have seen what a laugh can do. It can transform almost
unbearable tears into something bearable, even hopeful.

BOB HOPE

One of the things I learned the hard way was that it
doesn't pay to get discouraged.
Keeping busy and making optimism a way of life
can restore your faith in yourself.

LUCILLE BALL

I have never been disabled in my dreams.

CHRISTOPHER REEVE

Keep your face to the sunshine
and you cannot see the shadow.

HELEN KELLER

The "crisis" of yesterday is the joke of tomorrow.

H. G. WELLS

D

DATING, MARRIAGE, & DIVORCE

dat•ing *v* to go on a date with
mar•riage *n* legal union of a man
and woman as husband and wife
di•vorce *n* legal dissolution of a marriage

When you're first single, you're so optimistic. At the
beginning, you're like: "I want to meet a guy who's really
smart, really sweet, really good-looking, has a really great
career.". . . Six months later, you're like: "Lord—any
mammal with a day job."

CAROL LEIFER

I was out on a date recently and the guy took
me horseback riding. That was kind of fun,
until we ran out of quarters.

SUSIE LOUCKS

Do you know the best way for a guy to impress a girl at
the gym? The best way is to do pull-ups. . .pull up in a
Corvette, pull up in a Rolls-Royce, pull up in a Cadillac.

CONAN O'BRIEN

When I'm dating I look at a guy and wonder, "Is this the
man I want my children to spend their weekends with?"

RITA RUDNER

Let's face it, a date is like a job interview that lasts all
night. The only difference between the two is that there
are very few job interviews where there's a chance
you will end up naked at the end of it.

JERRY SEINFELD

Personally, I think if a woman hasn't met the right man
by the time she's 24, she may be lucky.

DEBORAH KERR

A girl can wait for the right man to come along but in
the meantime that still doesn't mean she can't have a
wonderful time
with all the wrong ones.

CHER

I just broke up with someone and the last thing she said
to me was, "You'll never find anyone like me again!"
I'm thinking, "I should hope not! If I don't want you,
why would I want someone like you?"

LARRY MILLER

My boyfriend and I broke up.
He wanted to get married and I didn't want him to.

RITA RUDNER

Marriage is a great institution,
but I'm not ready for an institution yet.

MAE WEST

In Hollywood a marriage is a success if it outlasts milk.

RITA RUDNER

Marriage is the alliance of two people, one of whom
never remembers birthdays and the other who never
forgets them.

OGDEN NASH

Marriage is not just spiritual communion and passionate
embraces; marriage is also three-meals-a-day
and remembering to carry out the trash.
JOYCE BROTHERS

A successful marriage requires falling in love many times,
always with the same person.
MIGNON MCLAUGHLIN

If marriage is your object,
you'd better start loving your subject.
ANONYMOUS

All marriages are happy.
It's trying to live together afterwards
that causes all the problems.
SHELLEY WINTERS

There's only one way to have a happy marriage
and as soon as I learn what is it I'll get married again.
CLINT EASTWOOD

I'd marry again if I found a man who had fifteen million
dollars, would sign over half to me,
and guarantee that he'd be dead within a year.
BETTE DAVIS

An archeologist is the best husband a woman can have;
the older she gets, the more interested he is in her.
AGATHA CHRISTIE

Husbands are like fires.
They go out if unattended.
ZSA ZSA GABOR

Only two things are necessary
to keep one's wife happy.
One is to let her think she is
having her own way,
and the other,
to let her have it.

LYNDON B. JOHNSON

The best way to get most husbands to do something
is to suggest that perhaps they're too old to do it.
SHIRLEY MACLAINE

The reason husbands and wives do not understand each
other is because they belong to different sexes.
DOROTHY DIX

Marrying a man is like buying something you've been
admiring for a long time in a shop window. You may love
it when you get it home, but it doesn't always go with
everything else.
JEAN KERR

My parents want me to get married. They don't care who
anymore as long as he doesn't have a pierced ear, that's
all they care about. I think men who have a pierced ear
are better prepared for marriage. They've experienced
pain and bought jewelry.
RITA RUDNER

I've always said we got married
because there was nothing on TV.

BETTE MIDLER

Getting divorced just because you don't love a man is
almost as silly as getting married just because you do.

ZSA ZSA GABOR

It wasn't exactly a divorce—I was traded.

TIM CONWAY

I've never married, but I tell people I'm divorced
so they won't think something's wrong with me.

ELAYNE BOOSLER

Divorce: A fifty-fifty settlement of the property, where
one gets the house and the other gets the mortgage.

EVAN ESAR

In Hollywood, an equitable divorce settlement means
each party getting fifty percent of publicity.

LAUREN BACALL

One reason people get divorced
is that they run out of gift ideas.

ROBERT BYRNE

Being divorced is like being hit by a Mack truck—
if you survive you start looking very
carefully to the right and left.

JEAN KERR

For a while, we pondered whether
to take a vacation or get a divorce.
We decided that a trip to Bermuda is over
in two weeks, but a divorce is something
you always have.

WOODY ALLEN

That's the only good thing about divorce.
You get to sleep with your mother.

ANITA LOOS

D

DEATH & DYING

death *n* termination of life
dy•ing *v* to cease living

It matters not how a man dies, but how he lives.

SAMUEL JOHNSON

The value of life lies not in the length of days,
but in the use we make of them;
a man may live long yet live very little.

MONTAIGNE

Death is not the greatest loss in life.
The greatest loss is what dies inside us while we live.

NORMAN COUSINS

Let us so live that when we come to die
even the undertaker will be sorry.

MARK TWAIN

There are worse things in life than death.
Have you ever spent and evening
with an insurance salesman?

WOODY ALLEN

Death: Nature's way of making you slow down.
EVAN ESAR

Death is nature's way of saying your table is ready.
ROBIN WILLIAMS

Death is nothing to fear. It is only another dimension.
WAYNE DYER

Death is simply a shedding of the physical body,
like the butterfly coming out of a cocoon. . . .
It's like putting away your winter coat when spring comes.
ELISABETH KÜBLER-ROSS

When one man dies, one chapter is not torn out of the
book, but translated into a better language.
JOHN DONNE

One of the situations in which everybody seems to fear
loneliness is death. In tones drenched with pity, people
say of someone, "He died alone." I have never understood
this point of view. Who wants to have to die and be polite
at the same time?

QUENTIN CRISP

It's not that I'm afraid to die,
I just don't want to be there when it happens.

WOODY ALLEN

If my doctor told me I only had six minutes to live,
I wouldn't brood. I'd type a little faster.

ISAAC ASIMOV

If you bemoan your brief stay on earth,
consider the mayfly which lives only for one day.
If the weather were bad that day,
your whole life could be rained out.

WES "SCOOP" NISKER

Everybody wants to go to heaven,
but nobody wants to die.
JOE LOUIS

Losing is the price we pay for living.
It is also the source of much of our growth and gain.
JUDITH VIORST

I think the most you can hope for at the end of life is that
your hair's messed, you're out of breath, and you didn't
throw up.
JERRY SEINFELD

We find by losing. We hold fast by letting go. We become
something new by ceasing to be something old. This
seems to be close to the heart of that mystery. I know
no more now than I ever did about the far side of death
as the last letting-go of all, but now I know that I do not
need to know, and that I do not need to be afraid of not
knowing. God knows. That is all that matters.
FREDERICK BUECHNER

To live in hearts we leave behind
is not to die.

THOMAS CAMPBELL

The highest tribute to the dead is not grief but gratitude.

THORNTON WILDER

To weep too much for the dead is to affront the living.

OLD SAYING

Weeping may endure for a night,
but joy cometh in the morning.

PSALMS 30:5

It is foolish to tear one's hair in grief,
as though sorrow would be made less by baldness.

CICERO

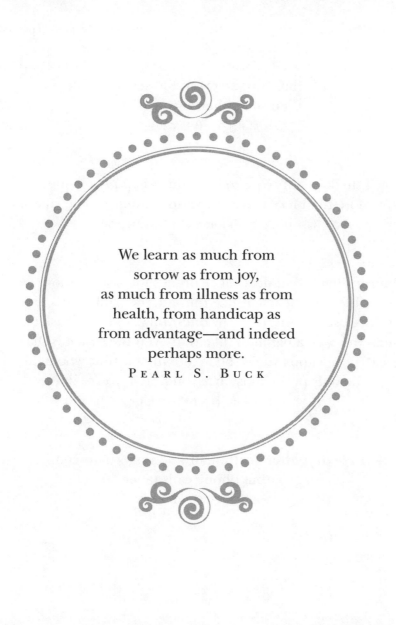

We learn as much from
sorrow as from joy,
as much from illness as from
health, from handicap as
from advantage—and indeed
perhaps more.

PEARL S. BUCK

If life must not be taken too seriously—
then so neither must death.
Samuel Butler

Life does not cease to be funny when people die
any more than it ceases to be serious when people laugh.
George Bernard Shaw

I mean that's what death is really, it's the last big move of
your life. The hearse is like the van, the pallbearers are
your close friends, the only ones you could really ask to
help you with a big move like that. And the casket is that
great, perfect box you've been looking for your whole life.
The only problem is once you find it, you're in it.
Jerry Seinfeld

For three days after death, hair and fingernails continue
to grow but phone calls taper off.
Johnny Carson

Of all the deathbed regrets that I have heard
not one of them has been,
"I wish I had spent more time at the office."
WAYNE DYER

Don't send me flowers when I die—give them to me now
so we can appreciate their beauty together!
C. LESLIE CHARLES

They say such nice things about people at their funerals
that it makes me sad to realize that I'm going to miss
mine by just a few days.
GARRISON KEILLOR

I did not attend his funeral, but I wrote a nice letter
saying I approved of it.
MARK TWAIN

They say you shouldn't say nothing about the dead unless
it's good. He's dead. Good.

M O M S   M A B L E Y

No matter how great a man is,
the size of his funeral usually depends on the weather.

R O S E M A R Y   C L O O N E Y

No matter who you are, you only get a little slice of the
world. Have you ever seen a hearse followed by a U-Haul?

B I L L Y   G R A H A M

The sight of a gravestone, weighty not only in its granite,
allows us perspective on problems as pressing as
burnt toast, taxes, and hay fever.

H A R R O W S M I T H   C O U N T R Y   L I F E

Of all escape mechanisms, death is the most efficient.

H .   L .   M E N C K E N

Death will be a great relief. No more interviews.
KATHERINE HEPBURN

·

I can't die yet. . .I'm booked!
GEORGE BURNS

I am ready to meet my Maker. Whether my Maker is
prepared for the ordeal of meeting me is another matter.
WINSTON CHURCHILL

I believe in sex and death—
two experiences that come once in a lifetime.
WOODY ALLEN

The only difference between sex and death is,
with death you can do it alone
and nobody's going to make fun of you.
WOODY ALLEN

I do not believe in an afterlife,
although I am bringing a change of underwear.

WOODY ALLEN

Eternity is a terrible thought. I mean,
where's it going to end?

TOM STOPPARD

If you die in the elevator,
be sure to push the UP button.

SAM LEVENSON

D

DIET & EXERCISE

di•et *v* to eat or drink according to a regulated system
ex•er•cise *n* activity that requires physical or mental exertion

One should eat to live, not live to eat.

MOLIÈRE

To lengthen thy Life, lessen thy meals.

BENJAMIN FRANKLIN

Never eat more than you can lift.

MISS PIGGY

Food is an important part of a balanced diet.

FRAN LEBOWITZ

I prefer Hostess fruit pies to pop-up toaster tarts because
they don't require so much cooking.

CARRIE SNOW

The two biggest sellers in any bookstore are the cookbooks and the diet books. The cookbooks tell you how to
prepare the food and the diet books tell you how not to
eat any of it.

ANDY ROONEY

This recipe is certainly silly. It says to separate two eggs,
but it doesn't say how far to separate them.

GRACIE ALLEN

Artichokes. . .are just plain annoying. . . .
After all the trouble you go to, you get about as much
actual "food" out of eating an artichoke as you would
from licking thirty or forty postage stamps. Have the
shrimp cocktail instead.

MISS PIGGY

I'm on a seafood diet. I see food and I eat it.

ANONYMOUS

I told my doctor I get very tired when I go on a diet,
so he gave me pep pills. Know what happened?
I ate faster.
JOE E. LEWIS

I've been on a diet for two weeks,
and all I've lost is two weeks.
TOTIE FIELDS

I've been on a constant diet for the last two decades.
I've lost a total of 789 pounds.
By all accounts, I should be hanging
from a charm bracelet.
ERMA BOMBECK

Eat, drink, and be merry, for tomorrow we diet!
ANONYMOUS

I never worry about diets.
The only carrots that interest me
are the number you get in a diamond.
M A E   W E S T

To feel "fit as a fiddle,"
you must tone down your middle.
A N O N Y M O U S

It's rough to go through life
with your contents looking as if
they settled during shipping!
M I L T O N   B E R L E

He who does not mind his belly,
will hardly mind anything else.
S A M U E L   J O H N S O N

When I buy cookies I just eat four and throw the rest
away. But first I spray them with Raid so I won't dig them
out of the garbage later. Be careful, though,
because that Raid really doesn't taste that bad.

JANETTE BARBER

I've decided that perhaps I'm bulimic
and just keep forgetting to purge.

PAULA POUNDSTONE

I did not become a vegetarian for my health.
I did it for the health of the chickens.

ISAAC BESHEVIS SINGER

Health food makes me sick.

CALVIN TRILLIN

Old people shouldn't eat health food.
They need all the preservatives they can get.

ROBERT ORBEN

You do live longer with bran
but you spend the last fifteen years on the toilet.
ALAN KING

The sovereign invigorator of the body is exercise,
and of all the exercises walking is the best.
THOMAS JEFFERSON

A vigorous five-mile walk will do more good for an
unhappy but otherwise healthy adult
than all the medicine and psychology in the world.
PAUL DUDLEY WHITE

I like long walks,
especially when they are taken by people
who annoy me.
FRED ALLEN

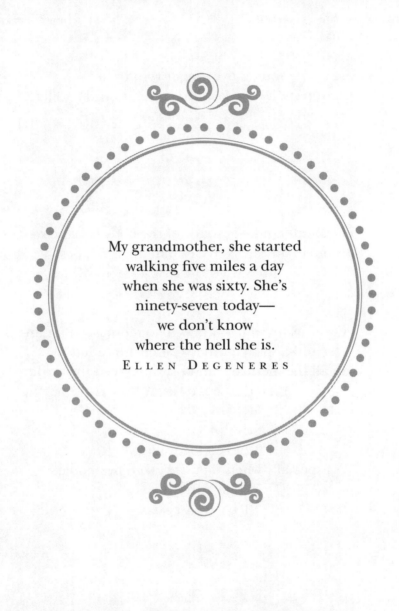

My grandmother, she started
walking five miles a day
when she was sixty. She's
ninety-seven today—
we don't know
where the hell she is.

ELLEN DEGENERES

You can't lose weight without exercise.
But I've got a philosophy about exercise.
I don't think you should punish your legs
for something your mouth did. Drag your lips
around the block once or twice.

GWEN OWEN

The only reason I would take up
jogging is so I could hear heavy breathing again.

ERMA BOMBECK

I have never taken any exercise
except sleeping and resting.

MARK TWAIN

When I feel like exercising
I just lie down until the feeling goes away.

ROBERT M. HUTCHINS

A bear, however hard he tries,
grows tubby without exercise.
POOH'S LITTLE INSTRUCTION BOOK,
INSPIRED BY A. A. MILNE

I've been doing leg lifts faithfully for about fifteen years,
and the only thing that has gotten thinner
is the carpet where I have been doing the leg lifts.
RITA RUDNER

Too many people confine their exercise to jumping
to conclusions, running up bills, stretching the truth,
bending over backward, lying down on the job, sidestep-
ping responsibility, and pushing their luck.
ANONYMOUS

I joined a health spa recently. They had a sign for "Free
Weights." So I took a couple.
SCOTT WOOD

Physical fitness is in. I recently
had a physical fit myself.
STEVE ALLEN

F

FRIENDS & FAMILY

friends *n* people who one knows; acquaintances
fam•i•ly *n* a group of persons sharing
common ancestry goals

The only way to have a friend
is to be one.
RALPH WALDO EMERSON

A man, Sir, should keep his friendship in constant repair.
SAMUEL JOHNSON

The best way to keep your friends
is not to give them away.
WILSON MIZNER

The best time to make friends is before you need them.
ETHEL BARRYMORE

Trouble is a sieve through which we sift our acquaintances. Those too big to pass through are our friends.
ARLENE FRANCIS

The essence of true friendship is to make allowances
for another's little lapses.
DAVID STOREY

A friend is a person who likes you for what you are,
in spite of all your faults, all your shortcomings.
ALFRED ARMAND MONTAPERT

In prosperity, our friends know us;
in adversity, we know our friends.
JOHN CHURTON COLLINS

Lots of people want to ride with you in the limo, but what
you want is someone who will take the bus with you
when the limo breaks down.
OPRAH WINFREY

A friend is someone who allows you distance
but is never far away.
NOAH benSHEA

A true friend is someone who is there for you
when he'd rather be anywhere else.
LEN WEIN

True friendship is seen through the heart
not through the eyes.
A N O N Y M O U S

If you are looking for a friend who has no faults,
you will have no friends.
H A S I D I C   F O L K   S A Y I N G

Laughter is not at all a bad beginning for a friendship,
and it is far the best ending for one.
O S C A R   W I L D E

The most valuable things in life are not
measured in monetary terms.
The really important things are
not houses and lands, stocks and bonds,
automobiles and real estate, but friendships,
trust, confidence, empathy, mercy, love, and faith.
B E R T R A N D   R U S S E L L   V .   D E L O N G

The holy passion of friendship is
of so sweet and steady and loyal and
enduring a nature that it will last through
a whole lifetime, if not asked to lend money.

MARK TWAIN

A friend costs nothing.
An enemy you must pay for.

YIDDISH FOLK SAYING

A friend is a person
who has the same enemies you have.

STEPHEN LEACOCK

A friend may well be reckoned the masterpiece of Nature.

RALPH WALDO EMERSON

Friendships multiply joy and divide griefs.

H. G. BOHN

My friends are my estate.

EMILY DICKINSON

A faithful friend is the medicine of life.

ECCLESIASTES 6:16

True friendship is like sound health,
the value of it is seldom known until it be lost.

CHARLES CALEB COLTON

Show me a genuine case of platonic friendship,
and I shall show you two old or homely faces.

AUSTIN O'MALLEY

Each friend represents a world in us,
a world possibly not born until they arrive,
and it is only by this meeting that a new world is born.

ANAIS NIN

Life's truest happiness is found in friendships we make
along the way.

ANONYMOUS

The happiest business in all the world is
that of making friends,
and no investment on the street pays
larger dividends, for life is more than
stocks and bonds, and love than rate percent,
and he who gives in friendship's name
shall reap what he has spent.

ANONYMOUS

There are three kinds of friends:
best friends, guest friends, and pest friends.

LAURENCE J. PETER

Man has three friends on whose company he relies.
First, wealth, which goes with him only while good
fortune lasts. Second, his relatives; they go only as far as
the grave, leave him there. The third friend, his good
deeds, go with him beyond the grave.

THE TALMUD

Friendship with oneself is all important because without
it one cannot be friends with anyone else in the world.

ELEANOR ROOSEVELT

A home-made friend wears longer
than one you buy in the market.

AUSTIN O'MALLEY

Think where man's glory most begins and ends,
And say my glory was I had such friends.

WILLIAM BUTLER YEATS

Two are better than one,
for if they fall, the one will lift up his fellow.

ECCLESIASTES 49:10

We are each of us angels with only one wing,
and we can only fly by embracing one another.

LUCIANO DE CRESCENZO

When a friend is in trouble,
don't annoy him by asking if there is anything
you can do. Think up something appropriate
and do it.

EDGAR WATSON HOWE

But friendship is precious,
not only in the shade,
but in the sunshine of life; and thanks
to a benevolent arrangement of things,
the greater part of life is sunshine.

THOMAS JEFFERSON

False friendship, like the ivy,
decays and ruins the walls it embraces;
but true friendship gives new life
and animation to the object it supports.

RICHARD BURTON

No man is useless while he has a friend.

ROBERT LOUIS STEVENSON

We need old friends to help us grow old
and new friends to help us stay young.

LETTY COTTON POGREBIN

In everyone's life, at some time, our inner fire goes out.
It is then burst into flame by an encounter with another
human being. We should all be thankful for those people
who rekindle the inner spirit.

ALBERT SCHWEITZER

One loyal friend is worth ten thousand relatives.

EURIPIDES

God gives us our relatives—
thank God we can choose our friends.

ETHEL WATTS MUMFORD

The family is one of nature's masterpieces.

GEORGE SANTAYANA

Family:
A social unit where the father is concerned
with parking space, the children with outer space,
and the mother with closet space.

EVAN ESAR

A family is a unit composed not only of children
but of men, women, an occasional animal, and the
common cold.

OGDEN NASH

If you cannot get rid of the family skeleton,
you may as well make it dance.

GEORGE BERNARD SHAW

The family you come from isn't as important
as the family you're going to have.

RING LARDNER

Happiness is having a large,
loving, caring, close-knit family in another city.

GEORGE BURNS

My mother loved children—
she would have given anything if I had been one.

GROUCHO MARX

Mother, food, love, and career:
the four major guilt groups.
CATHY GUISWITE

The most remarkable thing about my mother is that
for thirty years she served the family nothing but left-
overs. The original meal has never been found.
CALVIN TRILLIN

God could not be everywhere, so He created mothers.
LEOPOLD KOMPERT

I have found that no kisses can ever compare to "mom"
kisses, because mom kisses can heal anything.
You can have a hangnail, a broken heart, or catatonic
schizophrenia; with moms, one kiss and you're fine.
ROBERT G. LEE

H

HEALTH & HEALING

health *n* freedom from disease or abnormality
heal•ing *v* to restore to health

The secret of health for both mind and body
is not to mourn for the past, nor to worry
about the future, buy to live the present moment
wisely and earnestly.

BUDDHA

To be healthy, wealthy, happy, and successful in any and
all areas of your life you need to be aware that you need
to think healthy, wealthy, happy, and successful thoughts
twenty four hours a day and cancel all negative, destruc-
tive, fearful, and unhappy thoughts. These two types of
thought cannot coexist if you want to share in the abun-
dance that surrounds us all.

SIDNEY MADWED

Forgiveness is the way to true health and happiness.

GERALD JAMPOLSKY

Forgiveness is all-powerful. Forgiveness heals all ills.

CATHERINE PONDER

Always forgive your enemies;
nothing annoys them so much.
OSCAR WILDE

The healthy, strong individual
is the one who asks for help when he needs it.
Whether he has an abscess on his knee or in his soul.
RONA BARRETT

The best and most efficient pharmacy
is within your own system.
ROBERT C. PEALE

You don't get ulcers from what you eat.
You get them from what's eating you.
VICKI BAUM

Be careful about reading health books.
You may die of a misprint.
MARK TWAIN

It's no longer a question of staying healthy.
It's a question of finding a sickness you like.
JACKIE MASON

He's turned his life around. He used to be depressed and
miserable. Now he's miserable and depressed.

DAVID FROST

I moved to New York City for my health.
I'm paranoid and New York was the only place
where my fears were justified.

ANITA WEISS

When we hate our enemies, we are giving
them power over us: power over our sleep,
our appetites, our blood pressure, our health,
and our happiness. Our enemies would dance
with joy if only they knew how they were
worrying us, lacerating us, and getting even
with us! Our hate is not hurting them at all,
but our hate is turning our days and nights
into a hellish turmoil.

DALE CARNEGIE

There's a lot of people in this world
who spend so much time watching their health
that they haven't the time to enjoy it.

JOSH BILLINGS

Health is the condition of wisdom,
and the sign is cheerfulness—
an open and noble temper.

RALPH WALDO EMERSON

The simple truth is that happy people
generally don't get sick.

BERNIE S. SIEGEL

The body is the soul's house.
Shouldn't we therefore take care of our house
so that it doesn't fall into ruin?

PHILO

A man too busy to take care of his health
is like a mechanic too busy to take care of his tools.
S P A N I S H   S A Y I N G

If I'd known I was going to live this long,
I'd have taken better care of myself.
J I M M Y   D U R A N T E

Joy, temperance, and repose,
Slam the door on the doctor's nose.
H E N R Y   W A D S W O R T H   L O N G F E L L O W

Wondrous is the strength of cheerfulness,
and its power of endurance—the cheerful man will do
more in the same time, will do it better,
will preserve it longer, than the sad or sullen.
T H O M A S   C A R L Y L E

If your capacity to acquire has outstripped your capacity
to enjoy, you are on the way to the scrap-heap.
GLEN BUCK

Healing in its fullest sense requires looking into our
heart and expanding our awareness of who we are.
MITCHELL GAYNOR

When praying for healing,
ask great things of God and expect great
things from God. But let us seek for that healing
that which really matters, the healing of the heart,
enabling us to trust God simply,
face God honestly, and live triumphantly.
ARLO F. NEWELL

Our greatest healer is sitting right under our nose,
moving in and out—our breath.
JACQUELYN SMALL

The great secret of doctors,
known only to their wives, but still hidden from the
public, is that most things get better by themselves;
most things, in fact, are better in the morning.

LEWIS THOMAS

The greatest healing therapy is friendship and love.

HUBERT HUMPHREY

The mind is its own place, and in itself,
can make heaven of Hell, and a hell of Heaven.

JOHN MILTON

What your mind possesses your body expresses.

ANONYMOUS

When an emotional injury takes place,
the body begins a process as natural as the healing
of a physical wound. Let the process happen.
Trust that nature will do the healing.
Know that the pain will pass, and when it passes,
you will be stronger, happier,
more sensitive, and aware.

MELBA COLGROVE,
HAROLD H. BLOOMFIELD,
& PETER McWILLIAMS

No day is so bad it can't be fixed with a nap.

CARRIE SNOW

There must be quite a few things a hot bath won't cure,
but I don't know many of them.

SYLVIA PLATH

The power to heal is in you,
and nonetheless there is a tendency in our culture
to project onto other people and to want them to heal us.
ANDREW WEIL

Never go to a doctor whose office plants have died.
ERMA BOMBECK

My doctor said I look like a million dollars—
green and wrinkled.
RED SKELTON

Some people think that doctors and nurses
can put scrambled eggs back into the shell.
DOROTHY CANFIELD FISHER

A rule of thumb in the matter of medical advice
is to take everything any doctor says
with a grain of aspirin.
GOODMAN ACE

H

HOUSEKEEPING

house•keep•ing *n* performance of household tasks

I hate housework! You make the beds, you do the dishes,
and six months later you have to start all over again.

JOAN RIVERS

Cleaning your house while your kids are still growing
is like shoveling the walk before it stops snowing.

PHYLLIS DILLER

The darn trouble with cleaning the house is
it gets dirty the next day anyway,
so skip a week if you have to.
The children are the most important thing.

BARBARA BUSH

There is no need to do any housework at all.
After the first four years the dirt doesn't get any worse.

QUENTIN CRISP

I would rather lie on a sofa than sweep beneath it.

SHIRLEY CONRAN

The Rose Bowl is the only bowl I've ever seen
that I didn't have to clean.

ERMA BOMBECK

I'm a housewife. I'm not going to vacuum
'til Sears makes one you can ride on.

ROSEANNE

The toughest thing about being a housewife
is you have no place to stay home from.

PATRICIA C. BEUDOIN

I'm a great housekeeper.
I get divorced, I keep the house.

ZSA ZSA GABOR

Rich people do spring cleaning too.
Liz Taylor is completely exhausted after spraying
Windex on her diamonds.

KAREN LEE

Thank God for dirty dishes;
they have a tale to tell.
While other folks go hungry,
we're eating pretty well.
With home, and health, and happiness,
we shouldn't want to fuss;
For by this stack of evidence,
God's very good to us.

ANONYMOUS

There is such a build-up of crud in my oven
there is only room to bake a single cupcake.

PHYLLIS DILLER

I can't cook. I use a smoke alarm as a timer.

CAROL SISKIND

I tried to save grocery money once,
but some of the suggestions were just not practical,
like "Don't shop when you're hungry,"
which eliminated all hours when the store was open.
E R M A   B O M B E C K

Be it ever so humble, there's no place like home.
J O H N   H O W A R D   P A Y N E

A good laugh is sunshine in a house.
W I L L I A M   M A K E P E A C E   T H A C K E R A Y

K

KIDS

ba•bies n a very young child; an infant
chil•dren n a person between birth and puberty
teen•ag•ers n a person between the ages of 13 and 19

Babies are such a nice way to start people.

DON HEROLD

A baby is God's opinion that the world should go on.

CARL SANDBURG

When you are a mother, you are never really alone in
your thoughts. A mother always has to think twice,
once for herself and once for her child.

SOPHIA LOREN

Making the decision to have a child—it's wondrous.
It is to decide forever to have your heart
go walking around outside your body.

ELIZABETH STONE

It sometimes happens, even in the best of families,
that a baby is born. This is not necessarily cause for
alarm. The important thing is to keep your wits
about you and borrow some money.

ELINOR GOULDING SMITH

Life is a flame that is always burning itself out,
but it catches fire again every time a child is born.

GEORGE BERNARD SHAW

When the first baby laughed for the first time,
the laugh broke into a thousand pieces and they all went
skipping about, and that was the beginning of fairies.

J. M. BARRIE

Somewhere on this globe every ten seconds,
there is a woman giving birth to a child.
She must be found and stopped.

SAM LEVENSON

[On pregnancy] To me, life is tough enough
without having someone kick you from the inside.

RITA RUDNER

It takes the whole village to raise the child.

AFRICAN SAYING

Before I got married I had six theories about bringing up
children; now I have six children and no theories.

LORD ROCHESTER

A child is a curly, dimpled lunatic.

RALPH WALDO EMERSON

Raising children is a creative endeavor,
an art, rather than a science.

BRUNO BETTELHEIM

In automobile terms, the child supplies the power but
the parents have to do the steering.
BENJAMIN SPOCK

A child is the greatest poem ever known.
CHRISTOPHER MORLEY

Pretty much all the honest truth telling there is in the
world is done by children.
OLIVER WENDELL HOLMES

While we try to teach our children all about life,
our children teach us what life is all about.
ANGELA SCHWINDT

Seek the wisdom of the ages,
but look at the world through the eyes of a child.
RON WILD

There are children playing in the streets who could solve
some of my top problems in physics because they have
modes of sensory perception that I lost long ago.

J. ROBERT OPPENHEIMER

You don't know how much you don't know
until your children grow up and tell you
how much you don't know.

S. J. PERELMAN

Children ask better questions than adults.
"May I have a cookie?" "Why is the sky blue?" and
"What does a cow say?" are far more likely to elicit a
cheerful response than
"Where's your manuscript?"
"Why haven't you called?" and
"Who's your lawyer?"

FRAN LEBOWITZ

Hang around doggies and kids; they know how to play.

GEOFFREY GODBEY

Parents learn a lot from their children
about coping with life.
MURIEL SPARK

You can learn many things from children.
How much patience you have, for instance.
FRANKLIN P. JONES

Remember, when they have a tantrum,
don't have one of your own.
JUDITH KURIENSKY

If you listen carefully to children
you will have plenty about which to laugh.
STEVE ALLEN

Children have more need of models than of critics.
JOSEPH JOUBERT

If I could say just one thing to parents,
it would be simply that a child needs someone
who believes in him no matter what he does.

ALICE KELIHER

Never fear spoiling children
by making them too happy.
Happiness is the atmosphere
in which all good affections grow.

ANN ELIZA BRAY

The word no carries a lot more meaning
when spoken by a parent
who also knows how to say yes.

JOYCE MAYNARD

The words that a father speaks to his children in the
privacy of home are not heard by the world,
but, as in whispering-galleries, they are clearly heard
at the end and by posterity.

JEAN PAUL RICHTER

If you want children to improve,
let them overhear the nice things you say
about them to others.

H A I M   G I N O T T

Most kids hear what you say;
some kids do what you say;
but all kids do what you do.

K A T H L E E N   C A S E Y   T H E I S A

If a child is to keep alive his inborn
sense of wonder without any such gilt
from the fairies, he needs the companionship
of at least one adult who can share it,
rediscovering with him the joy, excitement,
and mystery of the world we live in.

R A C H E L   C A R S O N

The best thing to spend on your children is your time.

L O U I S E   H A R T

To help your children turn out well,
spend twice as much time with them
and half as much money.

H. JACKSON BROWN

Children in a family are like flowers in a bouquet;
there's always one determined to face in an opposite
direction from the way the arranger desires.

MARCELENE COX

Likely as not, the child you can do the least with
will do the most to make you proud.

MIGNON McLAUGHLIN

The way we know our kids are growing up:
The bite marks are higher.

PHYLLIS DILLER

There are times when
parenthood seems nothing
but feeding the mouth
that bites you.

PETER DE VRIES

I take my children everywhere,
but they always seem to find their way back home.
ROBERT ORBEN

We've had bad luck with our kids—
they've all grown up.
CHRISTOPHER MORLEY

The quickest way for a parent to get a child's attention
is to sit down and look comfortable.
LAN OLINGHOUSE

The best way to keep children home
is to make the home atmosphere pleasant—
and let the air out of their tires.
DOROTHY PARKER

It goes without saying that you should never have more
children than you have car windows.
ERMA BOMBECK

Never lend your car to anyone
to whom you have given birth.

ERMA BOMBECK

Anyone who thinks that the art of conversation is dead
ought to tell a child to go to bed.

ROBERT GALLAGHER

Any kid will run an errand for you,
if you ask him at bedtime.

RED SKELTON

I have found the best way to give advice
to your children is to find out what they want
and then advise them to do it.

HARRY S. TRUMAN

The easiest way to convince my kids
that they don't really need something
is to get it for them.

JOAN COLLINS

Grandchildren are God's way of compensating us
for growing old.
MARY H. WALDRIP

Be nice to your kids.
They choose your nursing home.
BUMPER STICKER

Adolescence is like cactus.
ANAIS NIN

Adolescence is that period in kids' lives
when their parents become more difficult.
RYAN O' NEAL

There's nothing wrong with teenagers
that reasoning with them won't aggravate.
ANONYMOUS

The teenagers ain't all bad.
I love 'em if nobody else does.
There ain't nothin' wrong with young people.
Jus' quit lyin' to 'em.
MOMS MABLEY

Teenagers travel in droves, packs, swarms. . . .
To the librarian, they're a gaggle of geese.
To the cook, they're a scourge of locusts.
To department stores they're a big beautiful
exaltation of larks. . . .
all lovely and loose and jingly.
BERNICE FITZ-GIBBON

Remember that as a teenager
you are at the last stage in your life when you will be
happy to hear that the phone is for you.

FRAN LEBOWITZ

Teenagers are hormones with feet.

MARSHA DOBLE

L

LIFE & LIVING

life *n* the state or condition of a living organism
liv•ing *n* the condition or action of maintaining life

Life is all memory, except for the one present moment
that goes by you so quickly you hardly catch it going.
TENNESSEE WILLIAMS

Life isn't a matter of milestones,
but of moments.
ROSE KENNEDY

I am beginning to learn that it is the sweet,
simple things of life
which are the real ones after all.
LAURA INGALLS WILDER

Sooner or later we all discover that the important
moments in life are not the advertised ones, not the
birthdays, the graduations, the weddings, not the great
goals achieved. The real milestones are less prepos-
sessing. They come to the door of memory unannounced,
stray dogs that amble in, sniff around a bit, and simply
never leave. Our lives are measured by these.
SUSAN B. ANTHONY

If I had my life to live over again, I would have more
actual troubles and less imaginary ones. Oh, I've had
my moments, and if I had to do it over again, I'd have
more of them. In fact, I'd try to have nothing else, just
moments, one after another.

NADINE STAIR

If I had to live my life again,
I'd make the same mistakes, only sooner.

TALLULAH BANKHEAD

If I had my life to live over,
I'd live over a delicatessen.

ANONYMOUS

Life is like a box of chocolates.

FORREST GUMP

Life is too short to stuff a mushroom.

SHIRLEY CONRAN

Life is better than death, I believe, if only because
it is less boring, and because it has fresh peaches in it.

ALICE WALKER

Life is far too important a thing
ever to talk seriously about.

OSCAR WILDE

Not a shred of evidence exists in favor
of the idea that life is serious.

BRENDAN GILL

Life is too tragic for sadness.
Let us rejoice.

EDWARD ABBEY

In every moment, the quality of your life is on the line.
In each, you are either fully alive or relatively dead.

DAN MILLMAN

Life is no brief candle to me.
It is a sort of splendid torch which I've
got hold of for the moment and I want to
make it burn as brightly as possible
before handing it on
to the future generations.

GEORGE BERNARD SHAW

Life is not so bad if you have plenty of luck, a good
physique, and not too much imagination.

CHRISTOPHER ISHERWOOD

Life is like a ten-speed bike.
Most of us have gears we never use.

CHARLES SCHULZ

Life is a great big canvas;
throw all the paint on it you can.

DANNY KAYE

Life is like a blanket too short.
You pull it up and your toes rebel,
you yank it down and shivers meander about your
shoulder; but cheerful folks manage to draw
their knees up and pass a very comfortable night.

MARION HOWARD

I am convinced that life is 10%
what happens to me
and 90% how I react to it.
CHARLES SWINDOLL

Life is not the way it's supposed to be.
It's the way it is.
The way you cope with it is
what makes the difference.
VIRGINIA SATIR

Remember, life is not what happens to you
but what you make of what happens to you.
Everyone dies, but not everyone fully lives.
Too many people are having
"near-life experiences."
ANONYMOUS

I think of life itself, now, as a wonderful play
that I've written for myself. . .And so my purpose
is to have the most fun playing my part.
SHIRLEY MACLAINE

If you're too busy to enjoy life, you're too busy.
JEFF DAVIDSON

Do not take life too seriously.
You will never get out of it alive.
ELBERT HUBBARD

All I can say about life is, Oh God, enjoy it!
BOB NEWHART

Life is a jest; and all things show it.
I thought so once; but now I know it.
JOHN GAY

Be glad of life because it gives you the chance to love,
and to work, and to play, and to look up at the stars.

HENRY VAN DYKE

One should sympathize with the joy,
the beauty, the color of life—
the less said about life's sores the better.

OSCAR WILDE

So much sadness exists in the world
that we are all under obligation to contribute
as much joy as lies within our powers.

JOHN SUTHERLAND BONNELL

It's a funny thing about life;
if you refuse to accept anything but the best,
you very often get it.

W. SOMERSET MAUGHAM

The happiness of your life depends upon
the quality of your thoughts.

MARCUS ANTONIUS

The greatest discovery of any generation is
that human beings can alter their lives
by altering their attitudes.

ALBERT SCHWEITZER

I realized that if what we call human nature
can be changed, then absolutely anything is possible.
From that moment, my life changed.

SHIRLEY MACLAINE

The grand essentials to happiness in this life
are something to do, something to love,
and something to hope for.

JOSEPH ADDISON

We act as though comfort and luxury
were the chief requirements of life,
when all that we need to make us really happy
is something to be enthusiastic about.
CHARLES KINGSLEY

Life is a paradise for those
who love many things with a passion.
LEO BUSCAGLIA

The secret of life is to have a task,
something you devote your entire life to,
something you bring everything to,
every minute of the day for the rest of your life.
And the most important thing is,
it must be something you cannot possibly do.
HENRY MOORE

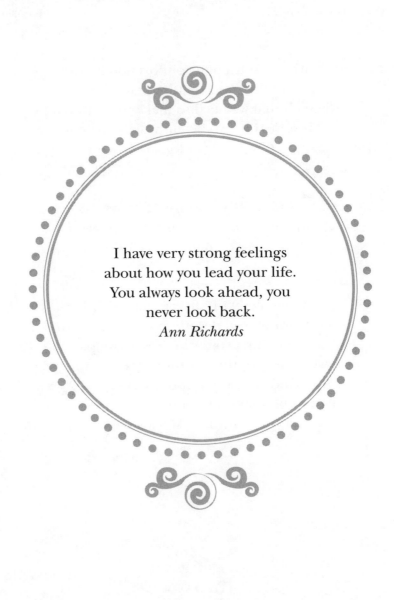

I have very strong feelings
about how you lead your life.
You always look ahead, you
never look back.
Ann Richards

Living in the past is a dull and lonely business;
looking back strains the neck muscles,
causes you to bump into people not going your way.

EDNA FERBER

Life is like playing a violin solo in public,
and learning the instrument as one goes on.

SAMUEL BUTLER

Life can only be understood backwards;
but it must be lived forwards.

SØREN KIERKEGAARD

Nobody gets to live life backward.
Look ahead—that's where your future lies.

ANN LANDERS

The best way to prepare for life is to begin to live.

ELBERT HUBBARD

If you want my final opinion on the mystery
of life and all that,
I can give it to you in a nutshell.
The universe is like a safe to which
there is a combination. But the combination
is locked up in the safe.

PETER DE VRIES

Life is the greatest of all bargains;
you get it for nothing.

YIDDISH SAYING

Life is something to do when you can't get to sleep.

FRAN LEBOWITZ

Life would be infinitely happier if we could only be born
at the age of eighty and gradually approach eighteen.

MARK TWAIN

Life:
Another game that is played with cards—
post-, greeting, punch, and credit.
EVAN ESAR

The purpose of life is a life of purpose.
ROBERT BYRNE

We make a living by what we get,
but we make a life by what we give.
WINSTON CHURCHILL

Only a life lived for others is a life worthwhile.
ALBERT EINSTEIN

When people are serving, life is no longer meaningless.
JOHN GARDNER

There must be more to life than having everything!

M A U R I C E   S E N D A K

The best advice I ever received was from a friend, who
once told me, "You can have anything you want.
You just can't have everything you want."

J O H N - R O G E R   &   P E T E R   M c W I L L I A M S

The best advice I've ever received?
How about the strangest?
When I was thirteen, my father took me aside
and told me that all a girl needed to know
to get by in life was written on the top of
a mayonnaise jar. I puzzled for days about
the meaning of the phrase,
"Refrigerate After Opening"—
until my father remarked that in his day
mayo jars always said,
"Keep Cool, Don't Freeze."

C .   E .   C R I M M I N S

In three words I can sum up
everything I've learned about life.
It goes on.

ROBERT FROST

Enjoy the little things in life, for one day you may look
back and realize they were the big things.

ANONYMOUS

One of the secrets of a happy life
is continuous small treats.

IRIS MURDOCH

My advice to you is not to inquire why or whither,
but just enjoy your ice cream while it's on your plate.

THORNTON WILDER

There are two things to aim at in life:
first, to get what you want; and, after that, to enjoy it.
Only the wisest of mankind achieve the second.
LOGAN PEARSALL SMITH

I finally figured out the only reason to be alive
is to enjoy it.
RITA MAE BROWN

I don't want to get to the end of my life and find
that I lived just the length of it.
I want to have lived the width of it as well.
DIANE ACKERMAN

Every day we should hear at least one little song,
read one good poem, see one exquisite picture,
and, if possible, speak a few sensible words.
JOHANN WOLFGANG VON GOETHE

Don't be afraid to go out on a limb.
That's where the fruit is.
H . JACKSON BROWN

Life engenders life. Energy creates energy.
It is by spending oneself that one becomes rich.
SARAH BERNHARDT

Look, I really don't want to wax philosophic,
but I will say that if you're alive,
you got to flap your arms and legs,
you got to jump around a lot,
you got to make a lot of noise,
because life is the very opposite of death.
And therefore, as I see it, if you're quiet,
you're not living. You've got to be noisy,
or at least your thoughts
should be noisy and colorful and lively.
MEL BROOKS

Live as if you expected to live a hundred years,
but might die tomorrow.
ANN LEE

Beginning today, treat everyone you meet
as if they were going to be dead by midnight.
Extend to them all the care, kindness,
and understanding you can muster, and do
with no thought of any reward.
Your life will never be the same again.
OG MANDINO

There are two ways of spreading light:
to be the candle or the mirror that reflects it.
EDITH WHARTON

Most of the shadows of this life are caused
by our standing in our own sunshine.
RALPH WALDO EMERSON

The world is a mirror: what looks in looks out.
It gives back only what you lend it.
LUDWIG BOEME

The follies which a person regrets most in his life are
those he didn't commit when he had the opportunity.
HELEN ROWLAND

Twenty years from now
you will be more disappointed by the things
you didn't do than by the ones you did.
So throw off the bowlines.
Sail away from the safe harbor.
Catch the trade winds in your sails.
Explore. Dream. Discover.
MARK TWAIN

First I was dying to finish high school and start college.
And then I was dying to finish college and start working.
And then I was dying to marry and have children to grow
old enough so I could return to work.
And then I was dying to retire.
And now, I am dying…
and suddenly realize I forgot to live.

A N O N Y M O U S

Live in such a way that you would not be ashamed
to sell your parrot to the town gossip.

W I L L   R O G E R S

There are only two ways to live your life.
One is as though nothing is a miracle.
The other is as though everything is a miracle.

A L B E R T   E I N S T E I N

It's all a miracle. I have adopted the technique
of living life from miracle to miracle.

A R T H U R   R U B I N S T E I N

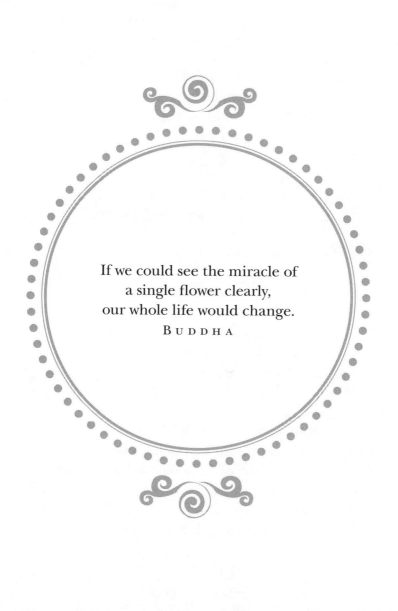

If we could see the miracle of
a single flower clearly,
our whole life would change.

B U D D H A

The art of being happy lies in the power
of extracting happiness
from common things.

HENRY WARD BEECHER

Anyone can be happy when times are good;
the richer experience is to be happy
when times are not.

SUSAN HARRIS

All the wonderful things in life are so simple
that one is not aware of their wonder
until they are beyond touch.

FRANCES GUNTHER

Lightness of touch and living in the moment are inter-
twined. One cannot dance well unless one is completely
in time with the music, not leaning back to the last step
or pressing forward to the next one, but poised directly
on the present step as it comes.

ANNE MORROW LINDBERGH

The moment you know how,
you begin to die a little.
The artist never entirely knows. We guess.
We may be wrong, but we take leap
after leap in the dark.

AGNES DE MILLE

We are not permitted to choose the frame of our destiny.
But what we put into it is ours.

DAG HAMMARSKJÖLD

You don't get to choose how you're going to die.
Or when. You can only decide
how you're going to live. Now.

JOAN BAEZ

Your only obligation in any lifetime
is to be true to yourself.

RICHARD BACH

Other people attempt to live their lives backwards;
they try to have more things or more money,
in order to do more of what they want,
so they will be happier. The way it actually works
is the reverse. You must first be who you really are,
then do what you need to do,
in order to have what you want.

M A R G A R E T   M E A D

Think of all the beauty still left around
you and be happy.

A N N E   F R A N K

There is nothing worse than being born
extraordinarily beautiful, nothing more
potentially damaging to the self.
You could say the same for being born
inordinately rich. You suddenly realize
how wise the idea is that you get nothing at
birth except things to transcend.
That's all you get.

M I L T O N   G L A S E R

I didn't belong as a kid,
and that always bothered me.
If only I'd known that one day
my differentness would be an asset,
then my early life would have been much easier.

BETTE MIDLER

He who has the why to live can bear
with almost any how.

FRIEDRICH NIETZSCHE

You are the creature of circumstance or the creator.

CAVETT ROBERT

Getting born is like being given a ticket
to the theatrical event called life. It's like going to the
theater. Now, all that ticket will get you, is through the
door. It doesn't get you a good time and it doesn't get you
a bad time. You go in and sit down and you either love
the show or you don't. If you do, terrific, and if you
don't—that's show business.

STEWART EMERY

Don't wait around for other people to be happy for you.
Any happiness you get you've got to make yourself.

ALICE WALKER

The last of human freedoms—
to choose one's attitude in any given set
of circumstances, to choose one's own way.

VICTOR FRANKL

If you can spend a perfectly useless afternoon in a
perfectly useless manner, you have learned how to live.

LIN YUTANG

M

MEN & WOMEN

men *n* adult male human beings
wom•en *n* adult female human beings

What is most beautiful in virile men
is something feminine;
what is most beautiful in feminine women
is something masculine.

SUSAN SONTAG

The ideal man has the strength of a male
and the compassion of a female.

ZOHAR

Women speak because they wish to speak,
whereas a man speaks only when driven to speech by
something outside himself—
like for instance, he can't find any clean socks.

JEAN KERR

Every man who is high up likes to think
he has done it all himself,
and the wife smiles and lets it go at that.
It's our only joke. Every woman knows that.

J. M. BARRIE

It's not the men in my life, but the life in my men.

MAE WEST

I never hated a man enough to give him diamonds back.

ZSA ZSA GABOR

If men can run the world, why can't they stop wearing
neckties? How intelligent is it to start the day
by tying a little noose around your neck?

LINDA ELLERBEE

Why are women wearing perfumes that smell like
flowers? Men don't like flowers.
I've been wearing a great scent.
It's called New Car Interior.

RITA RUDNER

Give a man a fish and he has food for a day;
teach him how to fish
and you can get rid of him for the entire weekend.
ZENNA SCHAFFER

Men aren't men
until they can get to Sears by themselves.
TIM ALLEN

If a woman gets nervous, she'll eat or go shopping. A man
will attack a country—it's a whole other way of thinking.
ELAYNE BOOSLER

Fighting is essentially a masculine idea;
a woman's weapon is her tongue.
HERMIONE GINGOLD

When men reach their sixties and retire, they go to
pieces. Women go right on cooking.

GAIL SHEEHY

Remember, Ginger Rogers did everything Fred Astaire
did, but she did it backwards and in high heels.

FAITH WHITTLESEY

I hate women because they always know
where things are.

JAMES THURBER

The people I'm furious with
are the Women's Liberationists.
They keep getting up on soapboxes
and proclaiming women are brighter than men.
That's true, but it should be kept quiet
or it ruins the whole racket.

ANITA LOOS

We women don't care too much about getting our
pictures on money as long as we can get our hands on it.
IVY (MAUDE) BAKER PRIEST

There's really nothing wrong with a woman welcoming
all men's advances, darling, as long as they are in cash.
ZSA ZSA GABOR

I bank at a women's bank.
It's closed three or four days a month due to cramps.
JUDY CARTER

The trouble with some women is they get all excited
about nothing—and then they marry him.
CHER

Women complain about sex more often than men.
Their gripes fall into two major categories:
(1) Not enough (2) Too much.
ANN LANDERS

Why does a woman work ten years
to change a man's habits and then complain
that he's not the man she married?

BARBRA STREISAND

The only time a woman really succeeds in changing a
man is when he's a baby.

NATALIE WOOD

Show me a woman who doesn't feel guilty
and I'll show you a man.

ERICA JONG

Sometimes I wonder if men and women
really suit each other. Perhaps they should live
next door and just visit now and then.

KATHARINE HEPBURN

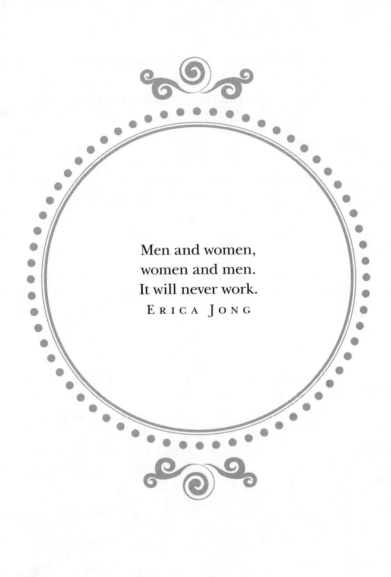

Men and women,
women and men.
It will never work.
ERICA JONG

M

MONEY MATTERS

mon•ey *n* official currency issued by a government

Money is better than poverty if only for financial reasons.
WOODY ALLEN

Money is a good thing to have.
It frees you from doing things you dislike.
Since I dislike doing nearly everything,
money is handy.
GROUCHO MARX

Money is relative. . .
the more money that rolls in the more the relatives.
ANONYMOUS

Money talks all right. Usually it says, "Good-bye."
ANONYMOUS

On income tax day I am reminded that while people say
money talks, mine seems to go without saying a word.
MARY ELLEN PINKHAM

I'm proud to pay taxes in the United States;
the only thing is, I could be just as proud
for half the money.

ARTHUR GODFREY

I believe we should all pay our tax bill with a smile.
I tried—but they wanted cash.

ANONYMOUS

It is more blessed to give than to receive.

ACTS 20:35

Not only is it more blessed to give than receive—
it is also deductible.

ANONYMOUS

Money doesn't always bring happiness. People with ten
million dollars are no happier than people with nine
million dollars.

HOBART BROWN

There's no reason to be the richest man in the cemetery.
You can't do any business from there.
C O L O N E L   S A N D E R S

I didn't want to be rich.
I just wanted enough to get the couch reupholstered.
K A T E   (M R S .   Z E R O)   M O S T E L

If you want to know how rich you really are,
find out what would be left of you tomorrow
if you should lose every dollar you own tonight.
W .   J .   B O E T C K E R

Measure wealth not by the things you have, but by the
things you have for which you would not take money.
A N O N Y M O U S

The man is the richest whose pleasures are the cheapest.
H E N R Y   D A V I D   T H O R E A U

The richest man in the world is not the one
who still has the first dollar he ever earned.
It's the man who still has his best friend.

MARTHA MASON

If you want an accounting of your worth,
count your friends.

MERRY BROWNE

What's money? A man is a success if he gets
up in the morning and goes to bed at night
and in between does what he wants to do.

BOB DYLAN

To fulfill a dream, to be allowed to sweat over lonely
labor, to be given a chance to create, is the meat and
potatoes of life. The money is gravy.

BETTE DAVIS

Not he who has much is rich,
but he who gives much.

ERICH FROMM

None are so poor that they have nothing to give...
and none are so rich that they have nothing to receive.

POPE JOHN PAUL II

There is enough in the world for everyone's need,
but not enough for everyone's greed.

FRANK BUCHMAN

Money is like water. When water is moving and flowing,
it cleanses, it purifies, it makes things green,
it's beautiful. But when it starts to slow down and sludge,
it becomes toxic and stagnant.

LYNNE TWIST

Money is like manure. If you
spread it around it does a lot
of good, but if you pile it up
in one place it stinks like hell.

CLINT MURCHISON

Money is just a fertilizer.
It can feed nightmares or dreams.
SHARON RIDDELL

When starting out, don't worry about
not having enough money. Limited funds are
a blessing, not a curse. Nothing encourages creative
thinking in quite the same way.
H. JACKSON BROWN

I thank fate for having made me born poor.
Poverty taught me the true value
of the gifts useful to life.
ANATOLE FRANCE

A poor person who is unhappy
is in a better position than a rich person
who is unhappy. Because the poor person has hope.
He thinks money would help.
JEAN KERR

Put not your trust in money,
but put your money in trust.
OLIVER WENDELL HOLMES

A lot of people will urge you to put some money in a
bank, and in fact—within reason—this is very good
advice. But don't go overboard. Remember, what you are
doing is giving your money to someone else to hold on to,
and I think that it is worth keeping in mind that the busi-
nessmen who run banks are so worried about holding on
to things that they put little chains on all their pens.
MISS PIGGY

I don't have a savings account because
I don't know my mother's maiden name.
PAULA POUNDSTONE

Never invest your money in anything
that eats or needs repairing.
BILLY ROSE

Invest in yourself, your family, your friends,
your planet, if you want a HIGH return.
SHARON RIDDELL

Invest in inflation.
It's the only thing going up.
WILL ROGERS

The safest way to double your money
is to fold it over once and put it in your pocket.
KIN HUBBARD

Money can't buy love—
but it certainly puts you in a wonderful
bargaining position.
HARRISON BAKER

Money can't buy friends,
but you can get a better class of enemy.
SPIKE MILLIGAN

Money won't buy happiness,
but it will pay the salaries of a large research staff
to study the problem.

BILL VAUGHAN

I see no point in money except to buy off anxiety.
I don't want to be rich. I want to be unanxious.

SIR JOHN BETJEMAN

Money is good for bribing yourself
through the inconveniences of life.

GOTTFRIED REINHARDT

The most popular labor-saving device is still money.

PHYLLIS GEORGE

If you want money, ask for money.
"I am enjoying the large sums of money that flow into my
life, quickly and effortlessly, this or something better for
my highest good and the highest good of all concerned."
JOHN-ROGER & PETER McWILLIAMS

Why is there always so much month
left at the end of the money?
ANONYMOUS

I couldn't be out of money. I still have checks.
ATTRIBUTED TO GRACIE ALLEN

The most beautiful words in the English
language are "Check Enclosed."
DOROTHY PARKER

It's good to have money and the things
that money can buy,
but it's good, too, to check up once in a while
and make sure that you haven't lost
the things that money can't buy.
GEORGE HORACE LORIMER

Certainly there are lots of things in life
that money won't buy, but it's very funny—
have you ever tried to buy them without money?
OGDEN NASH

I can't take it with me I know
but will it last until I go?
MARTHA F. NEWMEYER

Yesterday is a canceled check;
tomorrow is a promissory note;
today is the only cash you have.
Spend it wisely.
ANONYMOUS

P

PAIN & PLEASURE

pain *n* suffering or distress
pleas•ure *n* feeling of being pleased or gratified

Never a lip is curved with pain
that can't be kissed into smiles again.

BRET HARTE

The trick is not how much pain you feel—
but how much joy you feel. Any idiot can feel pain.
Life is full of excuses to feel pain,
excuses not to live, excuses, excuses, excuses.

ERICA JONG

Simply put, you believe that things
or people make you unhappy,
but this is not accurate.
You make yourself unhappy.

WAYNE DYER

What marks the artist
is his power to shape the material of pain we all have.

LIONEL TRILLING

You will not grow
if you sit in a beautiful flower garden,
but you will grow if you are sick,
in pain, experience losses, and
if you do not put your head in the sand,
but take the pain and learn to accept it,
not as a curse or punishment but as a gift to you
with a very, very specific purpose.

ELISABETH KÜBLER-ROSS

Pain is important:
how we evade it, how we succumb to it,
how we deal with it,
how we transcend it.

AUDRE LORDE

Those who have suffered understand suffering
and therefore extend their hand.

PATTI SMITH

I don't think of all the misery
but the beauty that still remains.
ANNE FRANK

We tire of those pleasures we take,
but never of those we give.
JOHN PETIT-SENN

Pleasure: an agreeable feeling caused
by getting the last laugh, having the last word,
or paying the last installment.
EVAN ESAR

Pleasure is the only thing to live for.
Nothing ages like happiness.
OSCAR WILDE

Why not seize the pleasure at once?
How often is happiness destroyed
by preparation, foolish preparation!

JANE AUSTEN

The great pleasure in life is doing
what people say you cannot do.

WALTER BAGEHOT

You find yourself refreshed
in the presence of cheerful people.
Why not make an honest effort
to confer that pleasure on others? Half the battle is
gained if you never allow yourself
to say anything gloomy.

LYDIA M. CHILD

One of the most lasting pleasures
you can experience is the feeling
that comes over you
when you genuinely forgive an enemy—
whether he knows it or not.

O .   A .   B A T T I S T A

Think big thoughts but relish small pleasures.

H .   J A C K S O N   B R O W N

S

STRESS & BURNOUT

stress *n* an upsetting condition caused
by adverse external influences
burn•out *n* physical or emotional exhaustion

The chief cause of stress is reality.

LILY TOMLIN

No one can escape stress,
but you can learn to cope with it.
Practice positive thinking…
seize control in small ways.

ADELE SCHEELE

I read this article. It said the typical symptoms
of stress are eating too much, smoking too much,
impulse buying, and driving too fast.
Are they kidding? This is my idea of a great day!

MONICA PIPER

Stress is the resistance to what's happening right now.
As we allow ourselves to open
to this moment fully, there is absolutely no stress.

STEPHAN RECHTSCHAFFEN

Stress is basically a disconnection
from the earth, a forgetting of the breath.
Stress is an ignorant state. It believes that
everything is an emergency.
Nothing is that important. Just lie down.
NATALIE GOLDBERG

Keep breathing.
SOPHIE TUCKER

Stress—that confusion created
when the mind must override the body's
basic desire to choke the living ****
out of some idiot
who desperately needs it.
OFFICE SIGN

Nothing is more destined to create deep-seated
anxieties in people than the false assumption
that life should be free from anxieties.
ARCHBISHOP FULTON J. SHEEN

If I knew what I was so
anxious about, I wouldn't be
so anxious.

MIGNON MCLAUGHLIN

Nothing erases unpleasant thoughts more effectively
than conscious concentration on pleasant ones.

HANS SELYE

If you can't help it, don't think about it.

CARMEL MYERS

For fast acting relief, try slowing down.

LILY TOMLIN

S

SUCCESS & FAILURE

success *n* the achievement of something desired
failure *n* not achieving the desired end

Success is never a destination—it's a journey.

SATENIG ST. MARIE

Success is that old ABC—ability, breaks, and courage.

CHARLES LUCKMAN

Success is simply a matter of luck. Ask any failure.

EARL WILSON

Success is often achieved
by those who don't know that failure is inevitable.

COCO CHANEL

Success to me is having ten honeydew melons
and eating only the top half of each one.

BARBRA STREISAND

Success has gone to my hips.

DOLLY PARTON

Life is a series of moments, to live each one is to succeed.
CORITA KENT

There is only one success—
to be able to spend your life in your own way.
CHRISTOPER MORLEY

Success has nothing to do with what you gain in life or
accomplish for yourself. It's what you do for others.
DANNY THOMAS

I must admit that I personally measure success in terms
of the contributions an individual makes to her or his
fellow human beings.
MARGARET MEAD

A true measure of your worth includes all the benefits
others have gained from your success.
CULLEN HIGHTOWER

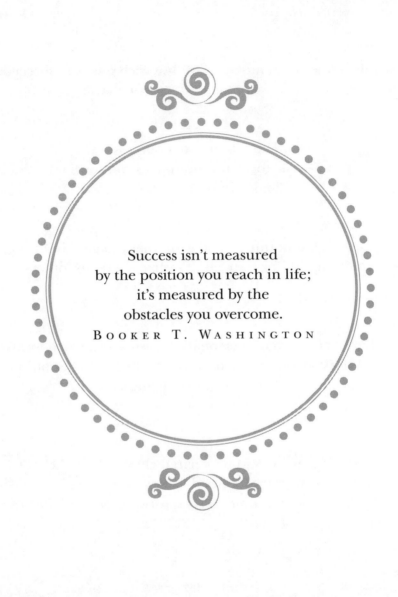

Success isn't measured
by the position you reach in life;
it's measured by the
obstacles you overcome.

BOOKER T. WASHINGTON

I owe my success to having listened respectfully
to the very best advice, and then going away
and doing the exact opposite.

G. K. CHESTERTON

If I wanted to become a tramp,
I would seek information and advice
from the most successful tramp I could find.
If I wanted to become a failure, I would seek advice
from men who have never succeeded. If I wanted to
succeed in all things, I would look around me
for those who are succeeding and do
as they have done.

JOSEPH MARSHALL WADE

Decide what you want,
decide what you are willing to exchange
for it. Establish your priorities and go to work.

H. L. HUNT

Be like a postage stamp—
stick to one thing till you get there.
JOSH BILLINGS

You can have anything you want
if you want it desperately enough.
You must want it with an inner exuberance
that erupts through the skin and joins
the energy that created the world.
SHEILA GRAHAM

To be successful, the first thing to do
is fall in love with your work.
SISTER MARY LAURETTA

If you don't do it excellently, don't do it at all.
Because if it's not excellent,
it won't be profitable or fun,
and if you're not in business for fun or profit,
what the hell are you doing there?
ROBERT TOWNSEND

What I wanted was to be allowed to do the thing
in the world that I did best—which I believed
then and believe now is the greatest privilege there is.
When I did that success found me.

DEBBI FIELDS

Make no little plans;
they have no magic to stir men's blood. . .
Make big plans, aim high in hope and work.

DANIEL H. BURNHAM

Don't be afraid to take a big step if one is indicated.
You can't cross a chasm in two small jumps.

DAVID LLOYD GEORGE

You can have big plans, but it's the
small choices that have the greatest power.
They draw us toward the future we want to create.

ROBERT COOPER

Far better it is to dare mighty things,
to win glorious triumphs even though checkered by fail-
ures, than to rank with those poor spirits
who neither enjoy nor suffer much because
they live in the gray twilight that knows
neither victory nor defeat.

THEODORE ROOSEVELT

Victory is won not in miles but in inches.
Win a little now, hold your ground, and later,
win a little more.

LOUIS L'AMOUR

Shoot for the moon.
Even if you miss it you will land among the stars.

LES BROWN

Some succeed because they are destined to;
most succeed because they are determined to.

ANATOLE FRANCE

When I thought I couldn't go on,
I forced myself to keep going.
My success is based on persistence, not luck.

ESTÉE LAUDER

Nothing in the world can take the place of persistence.
Talent will not; Genius will not;
Education will not;
Persistence and determination alone
are omnipotent.

CALVIN COOLIDGE

On the secret to success:
Early to bed, early to rise, work like hell,
and advertise.

GERTRUDE BOYLE

The only place you find success before work
is in the dictionary.

MAY V. SMITH

If at first you don't succeed
you're running about average.
M. H. ALDERSON

Success is getting what you want;
happiness is wanting what you get.
ANONYMOUS

That man is a success who has lived well,
laughed often, and loved much.
ROBERT LOUIS STEVENSON

Let no feeling of discouragement prey upon you,
and in the end you are sure to succeed.
ABRAHAM LINCOLN

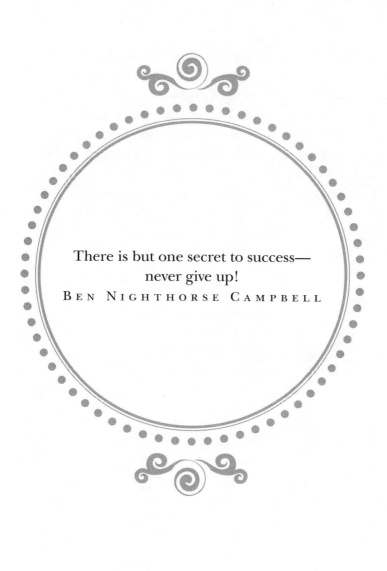

There is but one secret to success—
never give up!

BEN NIGHTHORSE CAMPBELL

To laugh often and much,
to win the respect of intelligent people
and the affection of children; to earn the
appreciation of honest critics and endure the
betrayal of false friends; to appreciate beauty;
to find the best in others; to leave the world a bit
better, whether by a healthy child, a garden patch, or a
redeemed social condition; to know even one life has
breathed easier because you have lived.
This is to have succeeded.

R A L P H   W A L D O   E M E R S O N

Success is a state of mind.
If you want success,
start thinking of yourself as a success.

J O Y C E   B R O T H E R S

If you have made mistakes…
there is always another chance for you…
you may have a fresh start any moment you choose,
for this thing we call "failure" is not the falling down,
but the staying down.

MARY PICKFORD

Only those who dare to fail greatly
can ever achieve greatly.

ROBERT KENNEDY

Our greatest glory is not in never failing,
but in rising up every time we fail.

RALPH WALDO EMERSON

Fall seven times, stand up eight.

JAPANESE SAYING

For every failure, there's an alternative
course of action. You just have to find it.
When you come to a roadblock, take a detour.

MARY KAY ASH

Failure is the opportunity to begin again
more intelligently.

HENRY FORD

There is much to be said for failure.
It is more interesting than success.

MAX BEERBOHM

To lose
Is to learn.

ANONYMOUS

Failure is success if we learn from it.

MALCOLM FORBES

Don't think of it as failure.
Think of it as time-released success.
ROBERT ORBEN

There is no failure except in no longer trying.
ELBERT HUBBARD

You may be disappointed if you fail,
but you are doomed if you don't try.
BEVERLY SILLS

Never let the fear of striking out get in your way.
BABE RUTH

Do not be afraid of defeat. You are never so near to
victory as when defeated in a good cause.
HENRY WARD BEECHER

Remember that a kick in the ass is a step forward.

ANONYMOUS

Act as though it were impossible to fail.

DOROTHEA BRANDE

Keep your eye on your heroes, not on your zeroes.

ROBERT H. SCHULLER

I don't know the key to success,
but the key to failure is trying to please everybody.

BILL COSBY

Quit now, you'll never make it.
If you disregard this advice, you'll be halfway there.

DAVID ZUCKER

If at first you don't succeed,
do it the way your wife told you to.
YVONNE KNEPPER

To those who need encouragement, remember this:
Beware of quitting too soon. Dr. Seuss' first children's
book was rejected by 23 publishers. The 24th publisher
sold 6 million copies.
ANN LANDERS

T

TIME & TECHNOLOGY

time *n* an interval separating two points of a continuum
tech•nol•o•gy *n* the scientific method used
to achieve an objective

Nothing is ours except time.

SENECA

Counting time is not so important as making time count.

JAMES J. WALKER

Time:
nature's way of preventing everything
from happening at once.

EVAN ESAR

You lose a lot of time hating people.

MARIAN ANDERSON

One always has time enough, if one will apply it well.

JOHANN WOLFGANG VON GOETHE

The time you enjoy wasting is not wasted time.

BERTRAND RUSSELL

Nothing puzzles me more than time and space;
and yet nothing troubles me less,
as I never think about them.
CHARLES LAMB

I never think of the future.
It comes soon enough.
ALBERT EINSTEIN

Time wounds all heels.
BENNETT CERF

I would I could stand on a busy corner, hat in hand, and
beg people to throw me all their wasted hours.
BERNARD BERENSON

If it weren't for Philo T. Farnsworth,
inventor of television,
we'd still be eating frozen radio dinners.
JOHNNY CARSON

If it weren't for electricity
we'd all be watching television by candlelight.
GEORGE GOBEL

Computers are useless.
They can only give you answers.
PABLO PICASSO

Television enables you to be entertained in your home
by people you wouldn't have in your home.
DAVID FROST

Thanks to television, for the first time the young are
seeing history made before it is censored by their elders.
MARGARET MEAD

I find television very
educational. Every time
someone turns on the set
I go into the other room
and read a book.

GROUCHO MARX

Television has proved that people will look at anything
rather than each other.

ANN LANDERS

There is no reason anyone would
want a computer in their home.

KEN OLSON,
FOUNDER OF DIGITAL EQUIPMENT CORP., 1977

I think there is a world market for maybe five computers.

THOMAS WATSON,
CHAIRMAN OF IBM, 1943

Computers in the future
may weigh no more than 1.5 tons.

POPULAR MECHANICS, 1949

Computers make it easy to do a lot of things,
but most of the things they make it easier to do,
don't need to be done.

ANDY ROONEY

To err is human, but to really foul things up
requires a computer.

ANONYMOUS

This telephone has too many shortcomings
to be seriously considered
as a means of communication.
The device is inherently of no value to us.

WESTERN UNION internal memo, 1876

Fax machine:
A device that allows someone in another state
to pile work on your desk.

MRS. WEBSTER'S GUIDE TO BUSINESS

One machine can do the work
of fifty ordinary men.
No machine can do the work
of one extraordinary man.
ELBERT HUBBARD

T

TRAVEL TROUBLES

trav•el *v* to go from one place to another

The journey, not the arrival, matters;
the voyage, not the landing.

PAUL THEROUX

It is good to have an end to journey towards;
but it is the journey that matters, in the end.

URSULA K. LEGUIN

To travel hopefully is a better thing than to arrive.

ROBERT LOUIS STEVENSON

Ride the horse in the direction that it's going.

WERNER ERHARD

It isn't how much time you spend somewhere that makes
it memorable; it's how you spend the time.

DAVID BRENNER

The really happy man
is one who can enjoy the scenery on a detour.

ANONYMOUS

Humor is the traveler's first line of defense.
Travel without humor is like sex without love.
You can do it, but what's the point really?

MARY MORRIS

The scientific theory I like best
is that the rings of Saturn
are composed entirely of lost airline luggage.

MARK RUSSELL

He who would travel happily must travel light.

ANTOINE DE SAINT-EXUPÉRY

I never travel without my diary.
One should always have something sensational to read.

OSCAR WILDE

It is easier to find a traveling companion
than to get rid of one.
ART BUCHWALD

Never play peek-a-boo with a child
on a long plane trip. There's no end to the game.
Finally I grabbed him by the bib and said,
"Look, it's always gonna be me!"
RITA RUDNER

A wise man travels to discover himself.
JAMES RUSSELL LOWELL

Though we travel the world over to find the beautiful,
we must carry it with us or we find it not.
RALPH WALDO EMERSON

Keep things on your trip in perspective, and you'll be
amazed at the perspective you'll gain on things back
home while you're away…. One's little world is put into
perspective by the bigger world out there.

GAIL RUBIN BERENY

A man travels the world over in search
of what he needs
and returns home to find it.

GEORGE MOORE

W

WORK WEARY

work *n* effort directed toward the accomplishment
of something

I never did a day's work in my life. It was all fun.

THOMAS EDISON

Nothing is really work
unless you would rather be doing something else.

J. M. BARRIE

In the long run you will receive more
from life doing the job you enjoy
than you will ever earn in money from a job you loath.

TERRY L. MAYFIELD

Do What You Love, the Money Will Follow
(book title)

MARSHA SINETAR

The secret of joy in work
is contained in one word—excellence.
To know how to do something well is to enjoy it.

PEARL S. BUCK

The supreme accomplishment is to blur the line
between work and play.
ARTHUR TOYNBEE

It is amazing how much people can get done
if they do not worry about who gets the credit.
SANDRA SWINNEY

Anyone can do any amount of work,
provided it isn't the work he is supposed
to be doing at that moment.
ROBERT BENCHLEY

I long to accomplish a great and noble task,
but it is my chief duty to accomplish small tasks
as if they were great and noble.
HELEN KELLER

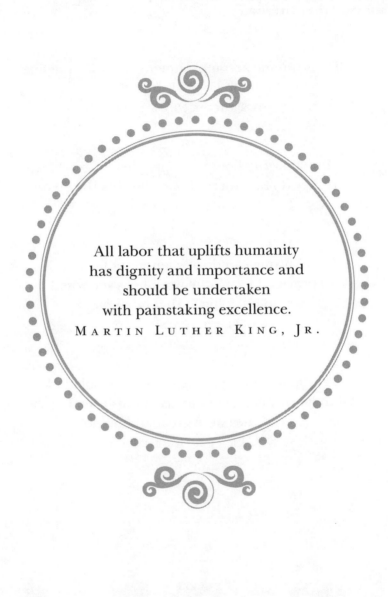

All labor that uplifts humanity
has dignity and importance and
should be undertaken
with painstaking excellence.

MARTIN LUTHER KING, JR.

Every morning I get up
and look through the *Forbes* list
of the richest people in America.
If I'm not there, I go to work.
ROBERT ORBEN

I don't have anything against work.
I just figure, why deprive somebody
who really loves it?
DOBIE GILLIS

Work is what you do so that some time
you won't have to do it anymore.
ALFRED POLGAR

Hard work never killed anybody, but why take a chance?
CHARLIE MCCARTHY (EDGAR BERGEN)

If you have a job without aggravations,
you don't have a job.
MALCOLM FORBES

The highest reward for a man's toil is not what he gets for
it but what he becomes by it.
JOHN RUSKIN

What makes you worthwhile is who you are,
not what you do.
MARIANNE WILLIAMS

Generate so much loving energy that people want to just
come and hang out with you. And when they show up,
bill them!
STUART WILDE

Occasionally indulging in a do-nothing day
is more than worth the price.
MALCOLM FORBES

W

WORRY WARTS

wor•ry *v* to feel concerned or uneasy about something

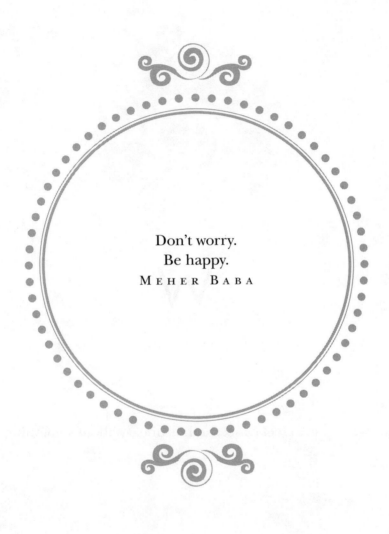

Don't worry.
Be happy.
MEHER BABA

Worry a little every day and in a lifetime
you will lose a couple of years.
If something is wrong, fix it if you can.
But train yourself not to worry.
Worry never fixes anything.
MARY HEMINGWAY

There is no good in arguing with the inevitable.
The only argument with an east wind
is to put on your overcoat.
JAMES RUSSELL LOWELL

Worry does not empty tomorrow of its sorrow,
it empties today of its joy.
ANONYMOUS

Don't waste the years struggling for things
that are unimportant. Don't destroy your peace of mind
by looking back, worrying about the past.
Live in the present, enjoy the present.
HENRY DAVID THOREAU

You're only here for a short visit.
Don't hurry, don't worry.
And be sure to smell the flowers along the way.
WALTER HAGEN

If you keep on saying things are going to be bad,
you have a good chance of being a prophet.
ISAAC BASHEVIS SINGER

Money is another pressure.
I'm not complaining, I'm just saying
that there's a certain luxury in having no money.
I spent ten years in New York not having it,
not worrying about it. Suddenly you have it,
then you worry, where is it going?
Am I doing the right thing with it?
DUSTIN HOFFMAN

You cannot prevent the birds of sorrow
from flying over your head, but you can prevent them
from building nests in your hair.

CHINESE SAYING

Walk away from it until you're stronger.
All your problems will be there when you get back,
but you'll be better able to cope.

LADY BIRD JOHNSON

When I look back on all the worries
I remember the story of the old man
who said on his deathbed
that he had had a lot of trouble in his life,
most of which never happened.

WINSTON CHURCHILL

What we anticipate seldom occurs;
what we least expect generally happens.

BENJAMIN DISRAELI

Worry often gives a small thing a big shadow.
SWEDISH SAYING

Worry is interest paid on trouble before it falls due.
DEAN INGE

The game is supposed to be fun.
If you have a bad day, don't worry about it.
You can't expect to get a hit every game.
YOGI BERRA

Most of my major disappointments
have turned out to be blessings in disguise.
So whenever anything bad does happen to me,
I kind of sit back and feel, well,
if I give this enough time, it'll turn out
that this was good,
so I shan't worry about it too much.
WILLIAM GAINES

Even in the deepest sinking
there is the hidden purpose of an ultimate rising.
Thus it is for all men, from none
is the source of light withheld unless
he himself withdraws from it.
Therefore the most important
thing is not to despair.

HASIDIC SAYING

My advice to actresses is don't worry about your looks.
The very thing that makes you unhappy
in your apprearance
may be the one thing to make you a star.

ESTELLE WINWOOD

You'll have a better day if you think about
where you're going rather
than what's stuck to the bottom of your shoes.

TAMMY HANSEN GILBERT

There are two days
about which nobody should ever worry,
and these are yesterday and tomorrow.

ROBERT J. BURDETTE

What, me worry?

ALFRED E. NEUMAN

INDEX TO AUTHORS

ABOUT THE AUTHOR

ALLEN KLEIN is an award-winning professional speaker and bestselling author. His first book, *The Healing Power of Humor*, which is now in its thirty-fifth printing and eighth foreign language translation, perfectly sums up his life-long philosophy—that humor is the best medicine for all ailments, big and small. A recipient of a Lifetime Achievement Award from the Association for Applied and Therapeutic Humor and an inductee into the Hunter College, New York City, Hall of Fame, Allen is also the world's one and only certified Jollytologist®, earning a Master's Degree from St. Mary's College in humor—no kidding! Nicknamed the "King of Whimsy," Allen has even worked in television production, designing children's television shows at CBS, including the beloved and wildly popular *Captain Kangaroo*. The author of fifteen uplifting and inspiring books, Allen currently resides and writes in San Francisco.

For more information about his books or presentations, go to www.allenklein.com or contact him at allen@allen-klein.com.